1

Table of Contents

I. Introduction

The *Real Estate Settlement Procedures Act (RESPA)* requires lenders and mortgage brokers to give you this booklet within three days of applying for a mortgage loan. RESPA is a federal law that helps protect consumers from unfair practices by settlement service providers during the home-buying and loan process.

Buying a home is an important financial decision that should be considered carefully. This booklet will help you become familiar with the various stages of the home-buying process, including deciding whether you are ready to buy a home, and providing factors to consider in determining how much you can afford to spend. You will learn about the sales agreement, how to use a *Good Faith Estimate* to shop for the best loan for you, required settlement services to close your loan, and the *HUD-1 Settlement Statement* that you will receive at closing.

This booklet will help you become familiar with how interest rates, points, balloon payments, and prepayment penalties can affect your monthly mortgage payments. In addition, there is important information about your loan after settlement, including how to resolve loan servicing problems with your lender, and steps you can take to avoid foreclosure. After you have purchased your home, this booklet will help you identify issues to consider before getting a home equity loan or refinancing your mortgage. Finally, contact information is provided to answer any questions you may have after reading this booklet. There is also a Glossary of Terms in the booklet's Appendix.

Using this booklet as your guide will help you avoid the pitfalls and help you achieve the joys of home ownership.

Purchasing Time-line

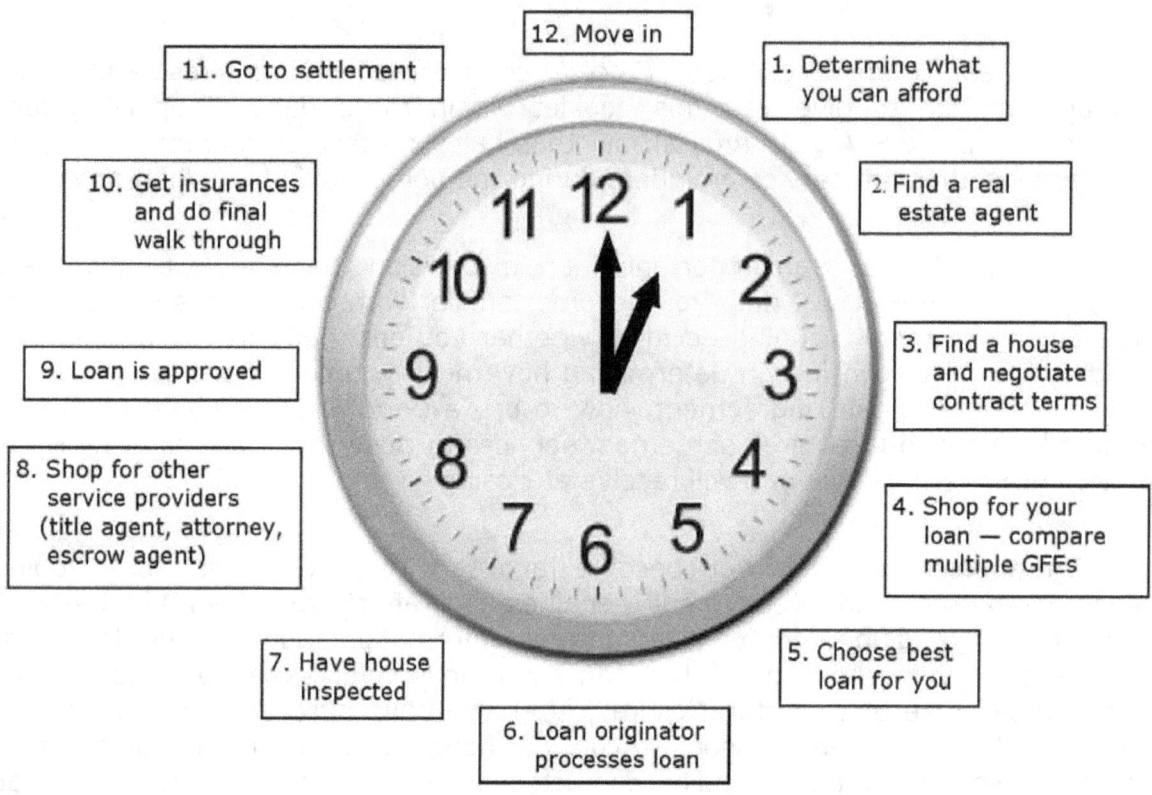

11. Go to settlement

12. Move in

1. Determine what you can afford

10. Get insurances and do final walk through

2. Find a real estate agent

9. Loan is approved

3. Find a house and negotiate contract terms

8. Shop for other service providers (title agent, attorney, escrow agent)

4. Shop for your loan — compare multiple GFEs

7. Have house inspected

6. Loan originator processes loan

5. Choose best loan for you

II. Before You Buy

Are You Ready to Be a Homeowner?

Buying a home is one of the most exciting events in your life and is likely to be the most expensive purchase that you will ever make. Before you make a commitment, make sure you are ready.

Avoid the pressure to buy a home that you cannot afford. Here are some things to consider:

➢ Are you ready to be a homeowner? It is critical that you consider whether you have saved enough money to support a down payment in addition to your other debts. You must have job stability and a steady income.

➢ How long do you plan on living in your home? Real estate is not always an investment. No one can predict what will happen with your local housing market. If you plan to sell your home in the next few years, realize that the property may not increase substantially in value or may have actually lost value. You may ultimately owe more to pay off your mortgage than your home will be worth.

➢ What is your estimated monthly payment for the home? In addition to the monthly payment for principal and interest, you will have to pay for taxes and insurance and possibly homeowner association dues. If your down payment is less than 20%, your lender may require that you pay the added expense for mortgage insurance.

➢ What are the other costs of owning a home? Be realistic about the costs of owning a home like heating and cooling and other utilities. You will generally need to budget for repairs and routine maintenance of your home, especially if you buy an older home.

➢ What can you afford? Be confident that you can make the monthly payments. Have a financial plan and make a budget. Do you have a steady source of reliable income to pay your mortgage should your interest rate increase in the future? Consider how many long-term debts you have such as car or student loans, as well as credit card bills.

➢ Have you talked with a housing counseling agency? Housing counselors can be very helpful, especially for first-time home buyers. The U.S. Department of Housing and Urban Development (HUD) supports housing counseling agencies throughout the country that can provide free or low-cost advice. You can search online at HUD's web site, or you can call HUD's interactive voice system. This contact information can be found in the Appendix of this booklet.

After answering the questions above, have you determined that buying a house is right for you? If so, congratulations! Let's start shopping for a house and a loan.

III. Determining What You Can Afford

To determine how much you can afford, you first need to know your monthly income. Second, you will need to calculate your monthly expenses which may include credit card bills, car payments, insurance premiums and all other debts. There is a worksheet in the Appendix **("Determining What You Can Afford Worksheet")** that will help you calculate your income and expenses to help determine what you can afford.

Consider talking with a financial professional such as a housing counselor to help you determine what you can afford. Keeping your payments affordable is the best way to avoid foreclosure or other financial difficulties. While mortgage lenders will tell you how much they are willing to lend you (which is the loan amount you "qualify" for), you probably know your finances better than anyone, so you should determine how much you are willing and able to pay every month for your home.

IV. Shopping for a House

Role of the Real Estate Agent or Broker

Frequently, the first person you consult about buying a home is a real estate agent or broker. Although these agents and brokers provide helpful advice, they may legally be representing the interests of the seller and not yours. You can ask your family and friends for recommendations.

It is your responsibility to search for an agent who will represent your interests in the real estate transaction. **If you want someone to represent only your interests, consider hiring an "exclusive buyer's agent", who will be working for you.**

Even if the real estate agent represents the seller, state laws usually require that you are treated fairly. If you have any questions concerning the behavior of an agent or broker, you should contact your State's Real Estate Commission or licensing department.

Sometimes, the real estate broker will offer to help you obtain a mortgage loan. He or she may also recommend that you deal with a particular lender, mortgage broker, title company, attorney, or settlement/closing agent. You are not required to follow the real estate broker's recommendation, and you should compare the costs and services offered by other providers before making a decision.

Role of an Attorney

Before you sign a sales agreement, you might consider asking an attorney to review it and tell you if it protects your interests. If you have already signed your sales agreement, you might still consider having an attorney review it.

If choosing an attorney, you should shop around and ask what services will be performed and whether the attorney is experienced in representing homebuyers. You may also wish to ask the attorney whether the attorney will represent anyone other than you in the transaction.

In some areas, an attorney will act as a settlement agent to handle your settlement.

Terms of the Sales Agreement

Before you sign a sales agreement, here are some important points to consider. While the real estate broker will probably give you a preprinted form of the sales agreement, many terms are negotiable so you may make changes or additions to the agreement. The seller, however, must agree to every change you make in order for such changes to be incorporated into the sales agreement.

For most home buyers, the sales price is the most important term. Make sure you know what the sales price includes, such as appliances. Here are other important terms of the sales agreement:

❖ **Mortgage Clause**

The mortgage clause will provide whether or not your deposit will be refunded if the sale is cancelled should you be unable to get a mortgage loan. Your agreement could allow the purchase to be canceled if you cannot obtain mortgage financing at or below a specific interest rate or through a specific loan program.

❖ **Settlement Costs**

You can negotiate which settlement costs you will pay and which will be paid by the seller. The seller may contribute a lump sum amount or may agree to pay for specific items on your behalf.

❖ **Inspections**

Most buyers prefer to pay for the following inspections so that the inspector is working for them, not the seller. You may want to include in your sales agreement the ability to cancel the agreement or renegotiate the contract for a lower sales price or for the needed repairs if you are not satisfied with the inspection results.

- o **Home Inspection:** You should have the home inspected. An inspection should determine the condition of the plumbing, heating, cooling and electrical systems. The structure should also be examined to assure it is sound and to determine the condition of the roof, siding, windows and doors. The lot should be graded away from the house so that water does not drain toward the house and into the basement. **You should be present to ask any questions.**

- o **Pests:** Your lender may require a certificate from a qualified inspector stating that the home is free from termites and other pests and pest damage. Even if your lender does not require a pest inspection, you may want to obtain a pest inspection to ensure the property does not have termites or other pests.

- o **Lead-Based Paint Hazards:** If you buy a home built before 1978, you have certain rights concerning lead-based paint and lead poisoning hazards. The seller or sales agent must give you the EPA pamphlet "Protect Your Family From Lead in Your Home" (or other EPA-approved lead hazard information). The seller must also disclose any known lead-based paint hazards in the property through a Lead Warning Statement and give you any relevant records or reports.

- o **Other Environmental Concerns:** Your city or state may require sellers to disclose known environmental hazards such as leaking underground oil tanks, the presence of radon or asbestos, lead water pipes, and other such hazards. You may want to determine the environmental condition of the home for your own safety. You could also be financially liable for the clean-up of any environmental hazards.

❖ **Sharing of Expenses**

You need to negotiate with the seller about how expenses related to the property such as taxes, water and sewer charges, condominium fees, and utility bills, are to be divided on the date of settlement. Unless you agree otherwise, you should only be responsible for the portion of these expenses owed after the date of sale.

Affiliated Businesses

When you are shopping for your home and your mortgage, a settlement service provider may refer you to its affiliated business. Affiliated business arrangements exist when several businesses are owned or controlled by a common corporate parent. When a lender, real estate broker, builder, or others refer you to an affiliated settlement service provider, RESPA requires that the referring party give you an Affiliated Business Arrangement Disclosure. **Except under certain circumstances, you are generally not required to use the affiliate and are free to shop for other service providers. You should shop around to determine that you are receiving the best service and rate.**

Builders

If you are buying a newly constructed home, a builder may offer you an incentive or "deal" if you select its affiliated mortgage company or other settlement service business. You should shop and compare interest rates and other settlement charges before entering a contractual agreement to use these affiliated companies.

V. Shopping for a Loan

Your choice of mortgage lender or broker, as well as type of loan itself, will influence your settlement costs and your monthly mortgage payment. You may find a listing of local lenders and mortgage brokers in the yellow pages and a listing of rates in your local newspaper. You may also wish to search the internet for lenders and brokers and their advertised rates. You can ask your family and friends about loan originators they have used and recommend.

Loan Originator

A loan originator is a lender or a mortgage broker.

- **Mortgage Brokers** Some companies, known as "mortgage brokers," offer to find you a mortgage lender willing to make you a loan. A mortgage broker may operate as an independent business and may not be operating as your "agent" or representative.

- **Lenders** A lender typically makes loans to borrowers directly. They receive payment through fees charged to you at settlement, payment from interest when you make your monthly mortgage payments and payments if they sell your loan or the servicing of your loan after settlement.

Note: Whether you apply for a loan with a lender or mortgage broker, you should receive *Good Faith Estimates* of settlement costs from multiple loan originators to make certain you get the best loan product at the lowest interest rate and lowest settlement costs.

Types of Loans and Programs

Shopping for your loan is probably the most important step in your home-buying process. Mortgage brokers and lenders have a wide variety of mortgage products. The type of loan product and your interest rate will not only influence your total settlement costs but will determine the amount of your monthly mortgage payment.

Government Programs

You may be eligible for a loan insured by the Federal Housing Administration (FHA), guaranteed by the Department of Veterans Affairs (VA) or offered by the Rural Housing Service (RHS). These programs usually require a smaller down payment. Ask your lender or mortgage broker about these programs. You should shop and compare quotes from different loan originators because each may offer different rates and loan terms.

If you are a first time homebuyer, ask your real estate agent/broker and loan originator about the availability of local or state programs such as reductions in transfer taxes, special income tax deductions or state homestead exemption discounts.

Types of Mortgages

Two of the most common types of mortgage loans are fixed-rate mortgages and adjustable rate mortgages. The interest rate on a fixed-rate mortgage will remain the same for the entire life of your loan while the interest rate on an adjustable rate mortgage (ARM) may adjust at regular intervals and may be tied to an economic index, such as a rate for Treasury securities. When the interest rate on an ARM adjusts it may cause your payment to increase.

Some adjustable rate mortgages allow the borrower to pay either the "interest only" or less than the "interest only." In both options, none of the mortgage payment is applied towards the loan balance (principal). In a less than "interest only" option, the unpaid interest is added to your loan balance and you can owe more than the amount you initially borrowed. **<u>When the loan balance increases to the maximum amount the loan is "recast" and your loan payment may double or even triple</u>**. When faced with "payment shock," you may discover too late that the loan payments no longer fit within your budget and that the loan is difficult to refinance. **You may then be in danger of losing your home.**

WARNING: Choosing an ARM product could affect your ability to pay your mortgage in the future resulting in loan default or foreclosure. You need to become familiar with the features of ARM products to find the one that best fits your needs. If you decide to obtain an ARM, consider obtaining additional information. Additional information may be found by contacting the Federal Reserve Board. Contact information is given in the Appendix to this booklet.

Taxes and Insurance

In addition to the principal and interest portion of your mortgage payment, you will have to pay property taxes and insurance to protect the property in the event of disaster such as a fire or flood. Based on your down payment, you may also have to pay mortgage insurance. Your lender may require an escrow or impound account to pay these items with your monthly mortgage payment. If an escrow account is not required, you are responsible for making these payments.

Mortgage insurance may be required by your lender if your down payment is less than 20% of the purchase price. Mortgage insurance protects the lender if you default on your loan. You may be able to cancel mortgage insurance in the future based on certain criteria, such as paying down your loan balance to a certain amount. Before you commit to paying for mortgage insurance, find out the specific requirements for cancellation. Mortgage insurance should not be confused with mortgage life, credit life, or disability insurance that are designed to pay off a mortgage in the event of a borrower's death or disability. Your *Good Faith Estimate* should not have any charges for mortgage life, credit life, or disability insurance.

Homeowner's (hazard) insurance protects your property in the event of a loss such as fire. Many lenders require that you get a homeowner's policy before settlement.

Flood insurance will be required if the house is in a flood hazard area. After your loan is settled, if a change in flood insurance maps brings your home within a flood hazard area, your lender or servicer may require you to buy flood insurance at that time.

VI. Good Faith Estimate (GFE)

The GFE is a three page form designed to encourage you to shop for a mortgage loan and settlement services so you can determine which mortgage is best for you. It shows the loan terms and the settlement charges you will pay if you decide to go forward with the loan process and are approved for the loan. It explains which charges can change before your settlement and which charges must remain the same. It contains a shopping chart allowing you to easily compare multiple mortgage loans and settlement costs, making it easier for you to shop for the best loan. The GFE may be provided by a mortgage broker or the lender. Until they give you a GFE loan originators are only permitted to charge you for the cost of a credit report.

In the loan application process, the loan originator will need your name, Social Security number, gross monthly income, property address, estimate of the value of the property, and the amount of the mortgage loan you want to determine the GFE. Your Social Security number is used to obtain a credit report showing your credit history, including past and present debts and the timeliness of repayment.

Your GFE Step-by-Step

Page 1 of the GFE

Now let's go through the GFE step-by-step. The top of page 1 of the GFE shows the property address, your name and contact information and your loan originator's contact information.

Important Dates

1. The interest rate for this GFE is available through January 2, 2010 @ 4pm   After this time, the interest rate, some of your loan Origination Charges, and the monthly payment shown below can change until you lock your interest rate.

2. This estimate for all other settlement charges is available through January 22, 2010

3. After you lock your interest rate, you must go to settlement within 30 days (your rate lock period) to receive the locked interest rate.

4. You must lock the interest rate at least 15 days before settlement

The Important Dates section of the GFE includes key dates of which you should be aware.
Line 1 discloses the date and time the interest rate offer is good through.
Line 2 discloses the date "All Other Settlement Charges" is good through. This date must be open for at least 10 business days from the date the GFE was issued to allow you to shop for the best loan for you.
Line 3 discloses the interest rate lock time period, such as 30, 45 or 60 days, that the GFE was based on. It does not mean that your interest rate is locked.
Line 4 discloses the number of days prior to going to settlement that you must lock your interest rate.
Note: "Locking in" your rate and points at the time of application or during the processing of your loan will keep the interest rate and points from changing until the rate lock period expires.

Summary of Your Loan

Your initial loan amount is	$ 200,000.00
Your loan term is	30 years
Your initial interest rate is	5.0 %
Your initial monthly amount owed for principal, interest, and any mortgage insurance is	$ 1,173.00 per month
Can your interest rate rise?	☐ No ☒ Yes, it can rise to a maximum of 10.0 %. The first change will be in 6 months
Even if you make payments on time, can your loan balance rise?	☒ No ☐ Yes, it can rise to a maximum of $
Even if you make payments on time, can your monthly amount owed for principal, interest, and any mortgage insurance rise?	☐ No ☒ Yes, the first increase can be in 6 months and the monthly amount owed can rise to $ 1,290.00 . The maximum it can ever rise to is $ 1,842.00 .
Does your loan have a prepayment penalty?	☒ No ☐ Yes, your maximum prepayment penalty is $
Does your loan have a balloon payment?	☒ No ☐ Yes, you have a balloon payment of $ due in years.

The Summary of Your Loan Terms discloses your loan amount, loan term, the initial interest rate and the principal, interest and mortgage insurance portion of your monthly mortgage payment. It also informs you if your interest rate can increase, if your loan balance can rise, whether your mortgage payment can rise and if there is a prepayment penalty or balloon payment.

In the example above, the loan amount is $200,000 which will be paid over 30 years. The initial interest rate is 5 percent and the initial monthly mortgage payment is $1,173 which includes mortgage insurance, but <u>does not include any amounts to pay for property taxes and homeowner's insurances if required by the lender.</u>

In our example, the loan has an adjustable interest rate. Since the interest rate can rise, the 'yes' box was checked, and the loan originator disclosed that the initial interest rate of 5 percent could rise as high as 10 percent. The first time your interest rate could rise is 6 months after settlement which could increase your payments to $1,290. Over the life of your loan your monthly payments could increase from $1,173 to $1,842.

This example does not contain a balloon payment or a prepayment penalty.

NOTE: A prepayment penalty is a charge that is assessed if you pay off the loan within a specified time period, such as three years. A balloon payment is due on a mortgage that usually offers a low monthly payment for an initial period of time. After that period of time elapses, the balance must be paid by the borrower, or the amount must be refinanced. You should think carefully before agreeing to these kinds of mortgage loans. If you are unable to refinance or pay the balance of the loan, you could put your home at risk.

Escrow Account Information

Some lenders require an escrow account to hold funds for paying property taxes or other property-related charges in addition to your monthly amount owed of $ | 1,173.00 | .
Do we require you to have an escrow account for your loan?

[ ] No, you do not have an escrow account. You must pay these charges directly when due.

[X] Yes, you have an escrow account. It may or may not cover all of these charges. Ask us.

The GFE also includes a separate section referred to as "Escrow account information," which indicates whether or not an escrow account is required. This account holds funds needed to pay property taxes, homeowner's insurance, flood insurance (if required by your lender) or other property-related charges.

If the GFE specifies that you will have an escrow account, you will probably have to pay an initial amount at settlement to start the account and an additional amount with each month's regular payment. If you wish to pay your property taxes and insurance directly, some lenders will give you a higher interest rate or charge you a fee. **If your lender does not require an escrow account, you must pay these items directly when they are due.**

Summary of Your Settlement Charges

A	Your Adjusted Origination Charges (See page 2.)	$3,750.00
B	Your Charges for All Other Settlement Services (See page 2.)	$4,530.00
A + B	Total Estimated Settlement Charges	$ 8,280.00

The final section on page 1 of the GFE contains the adjusted origination charges and the total estimated charges for other settlement services which are detailed on page 2. You should compare the "Total Estimated Settlement Charges" on several GFEs.

Page 2 of the GFE

The price of a home mortgage loan is stated in terms of an interest rate and settlement costs. Often, you can pay lower total settlement costs in exchange for a higher interest rate and vice versa. Ask your loan originator about different interest rates and settlement costs options.

Your Adjusted Origination Charges, Block A

1.	**Our origination charge** This charge is for getting this loan for you.	$6,750.00
2.	**Your credit or charge (points) for the specific interest rate chosen** ☐ The credit or charge for the interest rate of ⬚ % is included in "Our origination charge." (See item 1 above.) ☒ You receive a credit of $ `3,000.00` for this interest rate of `5.0` %. This credit **reduces** your settlement charges. ☐ You pay a charge of $ ⬚ for this interest rate of ⬚ %. This charge (points) **increases** your total settlement charges. The tradeoff table on page 3 shows that you can change your total settlement charges by choosing a different interest rate for this loan.	-$3,000.00
A	Your Adjusted Origination Charges	$ 3,750.00

Block 1, "Our origination charge" contains the lender's and the mortgage broker's charges and point(s) for originating your loan.

Block 2, "Your credit or charge point(s) for the specific interest rate chosen."

- If box 1 is checked, the credit or charge for the interest rate is part of the origination charge shown in Block 1.
- If box 2 is checked, you will pay a higher interest rate and receive a credit to reduce your adjusted origination charge and other settlement charges.
- If box 3 is checked, you will be paying point(s) to reduce your interest rate and, therefore, will pay higher adjusted origination charges.

Note: A point is equal to one percent of your loan amount.

After adding or subtracting Block 2 from Block 1, "Your Adjusted Origination Charge" is shown in Block A.

In the example shown, the origination charge is $6,750. No points were paid to reduce the interest rate. Instead, because of the interest rate chosen, the offer contains a $3,000 credit that reduces the adjusted origination charge to $3,750.

Your Charges for All Other Settlement Services, Blocks 3 through 11

In addition to the charges to originate your loan, there are other charges for services that will be required to get your mortgage. For some of the services, the loan originator will choose the company that performs the service (Block 3). The loan originator usually permits you to select the settlement service provider for "Title services and lender's title insurance" (Block 4). "Owner's title insurance" is also disclosed (Block 5). Other required services that you may shop for are included in "Required services that you can shop for" (Block 6).

<table>
<tr><td colspan="2">3. Required services that we select
These charges are for services we require to complete your settlement. We will choose the providers of these services.</td><td rowspan="2">$383.00</td></tr>
<tr><td>Service</td><td>Charge</td></tr>
</table>

3. Required services that we select These charges are for services we require to complete your settlement. We will choose the providers of these services.	$383.00
Service *Charge*	
Appraisal $275.00	
Credit report $40.00	
Flood certification $12.00	
Tax service $56.00	
4. Title services and lender's title insurance This charge includes the services of a title or settlement agent, for example, and title insurance to protect the lender, if required.	$1,275.00
5. Owner's title insurance You may purchase an owner's title insurance policy to protect your interest in the property.	$175.00
6. Required services that you can shop for These charges are for other services that are required to complete your settlement. We can identify providers of these services or you can shop for them yourself. Our estimates for providing these services are below. *Service* *Charge* Survey $250.00 Pest inspection $45.00	$295.00

Block 3 contains charges for required services for which the loan originator selects the settlement service provider. These are not "shoppable" services and often include items such as the property appraisal, credit report, flood certification, tax service and any required mortgage insurance.

Block 4 contains the charge for title services, the Lender's title insurance policy and the services of a title, settlement or escrow agent to conduct your settlement.

Block 5 contains the charge for an Owner's title insurance policy that protects your interests.

NOTE: Under RESPA, the seller may not require you, as a condition of the sale, to purchase title insurance from any particular title company.

Block 6 contains charges for required services for which you may shop for the provider. Some of these items may include a survey or pest inspection.

7. Government recording charges These charges are for state and local fees to record your loan and title documents.	$50.00
8. Transfer taxes These charges are for state and local fees on mortgages and home sales.	$1,368.00
9. Initial deposit for your escrow account This charge is held in an escrow account to pay future recurring charges on your property and includes ☒ all property taxes, ☒ all insurance, and ☐ other [ ] .	$306.00
10. Daily interest charges This charge is for the daily interest on your loan from the day of your settlement until the first day of the next month or the first day of your normal mortgage payment cycle. This amount is $ [28.00] per day for [1] days (if your settlement is [1/31/2010]).	$28.00
11. Homeowner's insurance This charge is for the insurance you must buy for the property to protect from a loss, such as fire. 　Policy　　　　　　　　　　　Charge Homeowner's insurance　　　　$650.00	$650.00

Block 7 contains charges by governmental entities to record the deed and documents related to the loan.

Block 8 contains charges by state and local governments for taxes related to the mortgage and transferring title to the property.

Block 9 contains the initial amount you will pay at settlement to start the escrow account, if required by the lender.

Block 10 contains the charge for the daily interest on the loan from the day of settlement to the first day of the following month.

Block 11 contains the annual charge for any insurance the lender requires to protect the property such as homeowner's insurance and flood insurance.

Total Estimated Settlement Charges

B	Your Charges for All Other Settlement Services	$ 4,530.00
A + B	Total Estimated Settlement Charges	$ 8,280.00

"Your charges for All Other Settlement Services", Blocks 3 through 11, are totaled in Block B. Blocks A and B are added together resulting in the total estimated settlement charges associated with getting the loan. These Blocks are carried forward to the bottom of page 1 of the GFE.

Page 3 of the GFE

Page 3 of the GFE contains important instructions and information that will help you shop for the best loan for you.

Understanding which charges can change at settlement

These charges cannot increase at settlement:	The total of these charges can increase up to 10% at settlement:	These charges can change at settlement:
■ Our origination charge ■ Your credit or charge (points) for the specific interest rate chosen *(after you lock in your interest rate)* ■ Your adjusted origination charges *(after you lock in your interest rate)* ■ Transfer taxes	■ Required services that we select ■ Title services and lender's title insurance *(if we select them or you use companies we identify)* ■ Owner's title insurance *(if you use companies we identify)* ■ Required services that you can shop for *(if you use companies we identify)* ■ Government recording charges	■ Required services that you can shop for (if you do not use companies we identify) ■ Title services and lender's title insurance (if you do not use companies we identify) ■ Owner's title insurance (if you do not use companies we identify) ■ Initial deposit for your escrow account ■ Daily interest charges ■ Homeowner's insurance

There are three different categories of charges that you will pay at closing: charges that cannot increase at settlement; charges that cannot increase <u>in total</u> more than 10%; and charges that can increase at settlement. You can use this as a guide to understand which charges can or cannot change. Compare your GFE to the actual charges listed on the *HUD-1 Settlement Statement* to ensure that your lender is not charging you more than permitted.

Written list of settlement service providers

A written list will be given to you with your GFE that includes all settlement services that you are required to have, and that you are allowed to shop for. You may select a provider from this list or you can choose your own qualified provider. If you choose a name from the written list provided, that charge is within the 10% tolerance category. If you select your own service provider, the 10% tolerance will not apply.

Even though you may find a better deal by selecting your own provider, you should choose the provider carefully as those charges could increase at settlement. If your loan originator fails to provide a list of settlement service providers, the 10% tolerance automatically applies.

Using the tradeoff table

	The loan in this GFE	The same loan with lower settlement charges	The same loan with a lower interest rate
Your initial loan amount	$ 200,000.00	$ 200,000.00	$ 200,000.00
Your initial interest rate [1]	5.0 %	6.0 %	4.5 %
Your initial monthly amount owed	$ 1,173.00	$ 1,299.00	$ 1,113.00
Change in the monthly amount owed from this GFE	No change	You will pay $ 126.00 **more** every month	You will pay $ 60.00 **less** every month
Change in the amount you will pay at settlement with this interest rate	No change	Your settlement charges will be **reduced** by $ 1,500.00	Your settlement charges will **increase** by $ 1,500.00
How much your total estimated settlement charges will be	$ 8,280.00	$ 6,780.00	$ 9,780.00

[1] For an adjustable rate loan, the comparisons above are for the initial interest rate before adjustments are made.

The "tradeoff table" on page 3 will help you understand how your loan payments can change if you pay more settlement charges and receive a lower interest rate or if you pay lower settlement charges and receive a higher interest rate.

The loan originator must complete the first column with information contained in the GFE. If the loan originator has the same loan product available with a higher or lower interest rate, the loan originator may choose to complete the remaining columns. If the second and third columns are not filled in, ask your loan originator if they have the same loan product with different interest rates.

Using the shopping chart

	This loan	Loan 2	Loan 3	Loan 4
Loan originator name	ABC Company	DEF Company	CS Company	
Initial loan amount	$200,000.00	$200,000.00	$200,000.00	
Loan term	30 years	30 years	30 years	
Initial interest rate	5.0%	5.0%	5.375%	
Initial monthly amount owed	$1,173.00	$1,173.00	$1,219.00	
Rate lock period	30 days	30 days	30 days	
Can interest rate rise?	yes	yes	yes	
Can loan balance rise?	no	no	no	
Can monthly amount owed rise?	yes	yes	yes	
Prepayment penalty?	no	no	no	
Balloon payment?	no	no	no	
Total Estimated Settlement Charges	$8,280.00	$8,309.00	$5,840.00	

You can use this chart to compare similar loans offered by different loan originators. Fill in each column with the information shown in the "Summary of your loan" section from the first page of all the GFEs you receive. Compare each offer and select the best loan for you.

After You Choose the Best Loan for You

After comparing several GFEs, select the best loan for you and notify the loan originator that you would like to proceed with the loan. Keep your *Good Faith Estimate* so you can compare it with the final settlement costs stated on your *HUD-1 Settlement Statement*. Ask the lender and settlement agent if there are any changes in fees between your GFE and your HUD-1 Settlement Statement. Some charges cannot be increased, and your lender must reimburse you if those charges were illegally increased.

New Home Purchases

If you are purchasing a new home that is being built or has not been built yet, your GFE could change. If the GFE can change, the loan originator must notify you that the GFE may be revised at any time up to 60 days before settlement. If you get a revised GFE, look at it to determine if the loan and settlement costs it discloses are the best for you.

Changed Circumstances

If there are changes involving your credit, the loan amount, the property value, or other information that was relied on in issuing the original GFE, a revised GFE may be issued. Only the charges affected by the changed circumstance may be revised.

VII. Shopping for Other Settlement Services

There are other settlement services that the lender will require for your loan. You may be able to shop for these services or you may choose providers identified on the written list you receive from the loan originator. If you select providers on the list, the charges shown on the GFE must be within the 10% tolerance. Even though selecting a settlement service provider that is not on the list nullifies the 10% tolerance, you still may be able to find a better deal by shopping and selecting a provider yourself. However, remember that those charges could increase at settlement.

Title Services and Settlement Agent

When you purchase your home, you receive "title" to the home. Certain title services will be required by your lender to protect against liens or claims on the property. Title services include the title search, examination of the title, preparation of a commitment to insure, conducting the settlement, and all administration and processing services that are involved within these services. Many lenders require a lender's title insurance policy to protect against loss resulting from claims by others against your new home. A lender's title insurance policy does not protect you.

If a title claim occurs, it can be financially devastating to an owner who is uninsured. **If you want to protect yourself from claims by others against your new home, you will need an owner's policy.**

To save money on title insurance, compare rates among various title insurance companies. If you are buying a newly constructed home, make certain your title insurance covers claims by contractors. These claims are known as "mechanics' liens" in some parts of the country. In many states, title insurance premium rates are filed with the state and may not be negotiable, but other title service related charges may be. Be sure to ask your title agent about any available discounts such as a reissue rate or a simultaneous issue discount.

Title services also include the services of a settlement agent. Settlement practices vary from locality to locality, and even within the same county or city. Depending on the locality, settlements may be conducted by lenders, title insurance companies, escrow companies or attorneys for the buyer or seller. In some parts of the country, a settlement may be conducted by an escrow agent. Unlike other types of settlement, the parties may not meet around a table to sign documents. Ask how your settlement will be handled.

Survey

Lenders or title insurance companies may require a survey to disclose the location of the property. The survey is a drawing of the property showing the location of the house and other improvements on the property. You may be able to avoid the cost of a new survey if you determine the company who previously surveyed the property and request an update. Check with your lender and title insurance company on whether an updated survey is acceptable.

Homeowner's Insurance

As a condition to settle, many lenders will require that you procure homeowner's insurance, flood insurance or other hazard insurance to protect the property from loss. Don't forget to shop for the best rates.

VIII. Your Settlement and HUD-1

You have determined what you can afford, found the right house and shopped for the best loan for you. After all the hard work, it is time to go to settlement, but don't forget to bring your GFE to compare with the charges listed on the *HUD-1 Settlement Statement*. It is a good idea to review your HUD-1 before your settlement. Let your settlement agent and lender know that you want to receive a completed HUD-1 at least one day prior to your settlement.

Settlement

Your settlement may be conducted by your lender or your title insurance company, an escrow company, your attorney or the seller's attorney. Regardless of who performs the settlement, there will be many important documents that you will need to sign. Make sure you carefully read and understand all the documents before you sign them. Do not be afraid to ask the lender any questions you have about your loan documents.

HUD-1 Settlement Statement

The *HUD-1 Settlement Statement* (HUD-1) is a form that lists all charges and credits to the borrower and seller in a transaction. You have the right under RESPA to inspect the *HUD-1 Settlement Statement* before settlement occurs. When you receive a copy of the HUD-1, compare it to your GFE. Ask the lender questions about any changes in fees between your GFE and the HUD-1. Your lender must reimburse you if a closing cost tolerance was violated.

Page 1 of the HUD-1

100 – 300 Series, Summary of Borrower's Transactions

The first page of the HUD-1 summarizes all of the charges and credits to the buyer and seller.

Line 101 is the contract sales price.

Line 103 is the total settlement charges from page 2.

Lines 106 to 112 lists items you are reimbursing the seller for that were already paid for by the seller, such as property taxes or homeowner association dues.

Line 120 is the total of the 100 series section and is the total amount you owe.

Lines 200 to 209 contain credits for items paid by you, such as the earnest money deposit and other credits from the seller and other parties.

Lines 210 to 219 are credits from the seller for items owed by the seller that are due after settlement.

Line 220 is the total of all credits from Lines 201 to 219. Subtract the amount on Line 220 from the amount on Line 120.

Line 303 is the amount you must bring to settlement or the amount you will receive.

J. Summary of Borrower's Transaction	
100. Gross Amount Due from Borrower	
101. Contract sales price	$210,000.00
102. Personal property	
103. Settlement charges to borrower (line 1400)	$8,044.00
104.	
105.	
Adjustment for items paid by seller in advance	
106. City/town taxes to	
107. County taxes to	
108. Assessments to	
109.	
110.	
111.	
112.	
120. Gross Amount Due from Borrower	$218,044.00
200. Amount Paid by or in Behalf of Borrower	
201. Deposit or earnest money	$2,000.00
202. Principal amount of new loan(s)	$200,000.00
203. Existing loan(s) taken subject to	
204.	
205.	
206. Seller closing cost credit	$2,000.00
207.	
208.	
209.	
Adjustments for items unpaid by seller	
210. City/town taxes to	
211. County taxes 1/1/2010 to 1/31/2010	$200.00
212. Assessments to	
213.	
214.	
215.	
216.	
217.	
218.	
219.	
220. Total Paid by/for Borrower	$204,200.00
300. Cash at Settlement from/to Borrower	
301. Gross amount due from borrower (line 120)	$218,044.00
302. Less amounts paid by/for borrower (line 220)	($204,200.00)
303. Cash [X] From [ ] To Borrower	$13,844.00

700 Series, Total Real Estate Broker Fees

700. Total Real Estate Broker Fees		Paid From Borrower's Funds at Settlement	Paid From Seller's Funds at Settlement
Division of commission (line 700) as follows :			
701. $ 6,000.00 to ABC Real Estate Co.			
702. $ 6,000.00 to XYZ Real Estate Co.			
703. Commission paid at settlement			$12,000.00

This section of the settlement statement shows the commissions paid to the real estate agents. There are no corresponding lines on the GFE because the lender does not require this service before you get your loan.

800 Series, Items Payable in Connection with Loan

800. Items Payable in Connection with Loan			
801. Our origination charge includes origination point(s) (1% or $2,000)	$6,750.00	(from GFE #1)	
802. Your credit or charge (points) for the specific interest rate chosen	- $3,000.00	(from GFE #2)	
803. Your adjusted origination charges		(from GFE #A)	$3,750.00

Line 801, "Our origination charge," lists the lender's and mortgage broker's charge for getting you the loan and references GFE Block 1. In this example, Line 801 designates an origination point of $2,000 for possible tax deductibility.

Line 802 lists either the charge for the interest rate (points) or a credit and references GFE Block 2.

Line 803 lists "Your adjusted origination charges." This amount is the sum of Lines 801 and 802 and references Block A on the GFE.

804. Appraisal fee to Appraisal Company	(from GFE #3)	$325.00
805. Credit report to Credit Report Company	(from GFE #3)	$40.00
806. Tax service to Tax Service Company	(from GFE #3)	$76.00
807. Flood certification to Flood Certification Company	(from GFE #3)	$12.00
808.		

Line 804 is the charge for the appraisal report prepared by an appraiser.

Line 805 is the fee for a credit report showing your credit history.

Line 806 is the fee paid to a tax service provider for information on the real estate property taxes.

Line 807 is the fee paid to the service providing information on whether the property is in a flood zone.

Lines 804, 805, 806 and 807 usually reference GFE Block 3.

Lines 808 and any additional lines are used to list other third party services required by your lender, including FHA or VA fees.

900 Series, Items Required by Lender to be Paid in Advance

900. Items Required by Lender to be Paid in Advance			
901. Daily interest charges from 1/31/2010 to 2/1/2010 @ $ 28.00 /day		(from GFE #10)	$28.00
902. Mortgage insurance premium for months to		(from GFE #3)	
903. Homeowner's insurance for 1 years to Insure-It ($600 P.O.C. by borrower)		(from GFE #11)	

These are charges which the lender requires to be prepaid at settlement.

Line 901 lists the daily interest charges collected for the period between the date of your settlement and the first day of the next month. This charge is disclosed in Block 10 of your GFE. In this example, the loan closed on 1/31/10, and the interest on the GFE was calculated with a 1/31/10 closing date so the charges are the same on both. This amount on Line 901 may differ from the amount on the GFE if the settlement date changes.

Line 902 lists the charge for any up-front mortgage insurance premium payment due at settlement. This is one of the charges disclosed in GFE Block 3 of your GFE. In this example, there is no payment due.

Line 903 is the charge for the homeowner's insurance policy and is one of the charges disclosed in Block 11 of your GFE. In the example, the homeowner's insurance was paid prior to the day of settlement so the charge is listed as "P.O.C. by borrower". P.O.C. stands for "Paid Outside of Closing". You typically have to bring a pre-paid insurance policy to your settlement.

1000 Series, Reserves Deposited with Lender

This series of the HUD-1 lists the amounts collected by the lender to be placed in your escrow account for future payments of items such as homeowner's insurance, mortgage insurance and property taxes. Line 1007 is an adjustment to make sure lenders are only collecting the maximum amount allowed by law. In this example, even though the first year's homeowner's insurance premium has already been paid, the lender has started escrowing money to pay the next bill.

1100 Series, Title Charges

Line 1101 lists the charge for all title services and the lender's title insurance policy. Title services includes any service involved with providing title insurance, such as title examination, preparing the title commitment, clearing the title to the property, preparing and issuing the title policies and conducting the settlement. These charges correspond to GFE Block 4.

Line 1102 is the amount of the settlement or closing fee if performed by a company different from the one providing title insurance. This charge is part of the charge listed in Line 1101.

Line 1103 lists the charge for the Owner's title insurance policy, if you decided to buy one. It corresponds to Block 5 of the GFE.

Line 1104 lists the charge for the Lender's title insurance policy which is part of the charge listed in Line 1101.

Line 1105 is the Lender's title policy limit. It often is lower than the value of the property because it only covers the amount of your lender's lien on your property.

Line 1106 lists the Owner's title policy limit. The liability limit of the owner's policy is typically the purchase price paid for the property.

Line 1107 lists the portion of the title insurance premiums retained by the title insurance agent.

Line 1108 lists the portion of the title insurance premiums retained by the underwriter.

1200 Series, Government Recording and Transfer Charges

1200. Government Recording and Transfer Charges					
1201. Government recording charges			(from GFE #7)	$50.00	
1202. Deed $ 25.00	Mortgage $ 25.00	Release $ 15.00			$15.00
1203. Transfer taxes			(from GFE #8)	$1,368.00	
1204. City/County tax/stamps	Deed $ 684.00	Mortgage $			
1205. State tax/stamps	Deed $ 684.00	Mortgage $			

Government recording charges listed in the 1200 series on the HUD-1 are charges paid to state and local governmental agencies to record important documents such as the deed and mortgage or deed of trust and transfer taxes to legally transfer property.

Line 1201 lists all government recording charges and corresponds to Block 7 of your GFE. This represents the cumulative amount the borrower is paying for government recording charges.

Line 1202 itemizes specific recording charges for the deed, the mortgage, and any releases of prior liens against your property shown in Line 1201. When the seller pays for an item, such as a release, the charge is listed in the seller's column.

In this example, the borrower is paying $50.00 of the recording charges, and the seller is paying $15.00. The total paid for the government recording charges was $65.00 (borrower $50.00 / seller $15.00).

Line 1203 lists the charge for transfer taxes. Transfer taxes are charged by state or local government to transfer real property or place a new lien (mortgage or deed of trust) on a property. This charge is listed in Block 8 of your GFE.

Lines 1204 and 1205 itemize the charges for transfer taxes listed in Line 1203.

Line 1206 can be used to list additional items related to recording or transfer charges.

In our example, the government recording charge that appeared in block 7 of the GFE was $50.00 which is illustrated in the column on line 1201 on the HUD-1.

Series 1300, Additional Settlement Charges

1300. Additional Settlement Charges			
1301. Required services that you can shop for		(from GFE #6)	$295.00
1302. Survey to Measure-It	$ 250.00		
1303. Pest inspection to Rid-A-Bug	$ 45.00		
1304. Home Warranty to Home Warranty Company			$300.00
1305.			
1400. Total Settlement Charges (enter on lines 103, Section J and 502, Section K)			$8,044.00

Line 1301 is the total of lender required services for which you chose the provider (other than title services). These services are itemized in the lines below 1301. These charges are listed in Block 6 of your GFE.

In addition to services the loan originator required there may be additional services that you chose. In our example, Line 1304 lists a homeowner's warranty to provide protection for your home's mechanical systems and appliances. A charge for a pest inspection or survey will appear as a line item in the 1300 series of the HUD-1, if the borrower elected to obtain an inspection or survey that was not a condition of the loan or required by the lender.

Line 1400 is the total of all charges listed in page 2 on the HUD-1 for the seller and you, the buyer. These totals are also listed on page 1 of the HUD-1. Your charges appear in Section J, Summary of the Borrower's Transaction, on Line 103. The seller's charges are listed in Section J, Summary of Seller's Transaction, on Line 502.

Page 3 of the HUD-1

The third page of the HUD-1 is made up of two sections: the Comparison Chart and the Loan Terms. The Comparison Chart will help you compare the charges disclosed on your GFE and the actual charges listed on page 2 of the HUD-1. The Loan Terms section can assure you that the loan you applied for is the loan you received at settlement. This section should compare with the "Summary of Your Loan" on page 1 of the GFE.

Comparison Chart

There are three categories in the Comparison Chart: charges that could not increase at settlement, charges that in total could not increase more than 10% and charges that could change. Compare the charges listed in the GFE column with the charges in the HUD-1 column. If the charges that cannot increase have increased or the total of the charges that cannot increase more than 10% have exceeded the 10% increase limit, the lender must reimburse you at settlement or within thirty (30) days after settlement.

Comparison of Good Faith Estimate (GFE) and HUD-1 Charrges		Good Faith Estimate	HUD-1
Charges That Cannot Increase	HUD-1 Line Number		
Our origination charge	# 801	$6,750.00	$6,750.00
Your credit or charge (points) for the specific interest rate chosen	# 802	-$3,000.00	-$3,000.00
Your adjusted origination charges	# 803	$3,750.00	$3,750.00
Transfer taxes	# 1203	$1,368.00	$1,368.00

Charges That In Total Cannot Increase More Than 10%		Good Faith Estimate	HUD-1
Government recording charges	# 1201	$50.00	$50.00
Appraisal	# 804	$275.00	$325.00
Credit report	# 805	$40.00	$40.00
Tax service fee	# 806	$56.00	$76.00
Flood certfication	# 807	$12.00	$12.00
Title services and lender's title insurance	# 1101	$1,275.00	$1,275.00
Owner's title insurance	# 1103	$175.00	$175.00
	#		
Total		$1,883.00	$1,953.00
Increase between GFE and HUD-1 Charges		$ 70 or	4 %

Charges That Can Change		Good Faith Estimate	HUD-1
Initial deposit for your escrow account	# 1001	$306.00	$350.00
Daily interest charges $ 28.00 /day	# 901	$28.00	$28.00
Homeowner's insurance	# 903	$650.00	$600.00
Survey	# 1302	$250.00	$250.00
Pest inspection	# 1303	$45.00	$45.00

In the example above, the "Charges That In Total Cannot Increase More Than 10%" were only increased by $70 or 4% and did not exceed the 10% tolerance. For the category "Charges That Can Change" in this example the borrower selected a pest inspection and survey provider that were not on the written list.

Loan Terms

Loan Terms	
Your initial loan amount is	$ 200,000.00
Your loan term is	30 years
Your initial interest rate is	5.0 %
Your initial monthly amount owed for principal, interest, and any mortgage insurance is	$ 1,173.00 includes [X] Principal [X] Interest [X] Mortgage Insurance
Can your interest rate rise?	[ ] No [X] Yes, it can rise to a maximum of 10.0 %. The first change will be on 6/1/2010 and can change again every 6 months after 6/1/2010 . Every change date, your interest rate can increase or decrease by 1.0 %. Over the life of the loan, your interest rate is guaranteed to never be lower than 5.0 % or higher than 10.0 %.
Even if you make payments on time, can your loan balance rise?	[X] No [ ] Yes, it can rise to a maximum of $
Even if you make payments on time, can your monthly amount owed for principal, interest, and mortgage insurance rise?	[ ] No [X] Yes, the first increase can be on 6/1/2010 and the monthly amount owed can rise to $ 1,290.00 . The maximum it can ever rise to is $ 1,842.00
Does your loan have a prepayment penalty?	[X] No [ ] Yes, your maximum prepayment penalty is $
Does your loan have a balloon payment?	[X] No [ ] Yes, you have a balloon payment of $ due in years on
Total monthly amount owed including escrow account payments	[ ] You do not have a monthly escrow payment for items, such as property taxes and homeowner's insurance. You must pay these items directly yourself. [X] You have an additional monthly escrow payment of $ 350.00 that results in a total initial monthly amount owed of $ 1,523.00 . This includes principal, interest, any mortagage insurance and any items checked below: [X] Property taxes [X] Homeowner's insurance [ ] Flood insurance [ ] [ ] [ ]

Note: If you have any questions about the Settlement Charges and Loan Terms listed on this form, please contact your lender.

The last section on the HUD-1 clearly sets forth the terms of your loan, including the loan amount, your interest rate and your monthly payments. It will also disclose the monthly escrow payment account information. It lets you know whether your interest rate, your loan balance or your monthly payments can increase and whether your loan has a prepayment penalty or a balloon payment. Look at this information carefully and make sure that you are getting the loan and the terms that were set forth in your GFE. **If the loan terms do not match the loan terms on your GFE or if you have questions, contact your lender before signing any documents.**

IX. Your Loan after Settlement

After settlement, RESPA requires that lenders give you disclosures concerning the servicing of your loan and any escrow account. RESPA also gives you certain protections in regard to the timely payment of your taxes and insurance.

Servicing and Escrow Disclosure Statements

The company that collects your mortgage payments is your loan servicer. This may not be your lender. When you apply for your loan or within three business days, RESPA requires that your lender or mortgage broker tell you in writing whether someone else may be servicing your loan. After your settlement, if your loan servicer transfers the servicing of your loan to a new servicer, RESPA requires that you be notified in writing at least fifteen (15) days before the transfer. The notice must tell you when the transfer is effective and when you will begin making payments to the new servicer. The notice letter must also give you the contact information for the new servicer as well as other important information about the servicing of your loan.

If your loan requires an escrow account, the servicer of your loan must give you an initial escrow account statement at your settlement or within the following forty-five (45) days. That form will show all of the payments which are expected to be deposited into your escrow account and all of the disbursements which are expected to be paid from the escrow account during the year. Your servicer will review your escrow account annually and send you a disclosure each year which shows the prior year's activity and any adjustments necessary in the escrow payments that need to be made in the upcoming year. You will not receive this yearly disclosure if your loan is in default. Remember that your monthly payment can increase if your taxes or insurance payments increase.

Servicing Errors

If you have a question any time during the life of your loan, RESPA requires the company collecting your loan payments (your "servicer") to respond to you. Write to your servicer and call it a "qualified written request under Section 6 of RESPA." A "qualified written request" (QWR) should be a separate letter and not mailed with the payment coupon. Describe the problem and include your name and account number. The servicer must investigate and make appropriate corrections within 60 business days.

Complaints

RESPA provides you with certain consumer protections during the loan process and during the servicing of your loan after settlement. If your lender charged you more than the allowable tolerances at settlement and failed to reimburse you; if you are aware that one of your settlement service providers paid or received a fee or kickback for referring business to someone; if you were required to use a company that was affiliated with your real estate agent, builder, or loan originator, if your loan servicer fails to timely pay your taxes and insurance premiums; or if your loan servicer does not respond to a QWR about the servicing of your loan, you may wish to file a complaint with HUD's Office of RESPA. You should describe what you believe to be a violation and identify each violator by name, address and phone number. You should also include your own contact information for any follow-up questions. You can find out how to file a complaint at the RESPA website or by contacting the RESPA Office. The address is located in the Appendix.

Avoiding Foreclosure

Once you move into your new home, you will want to make sure that you do nothing that could threaten you with the loss of your home. Make all payments on time. If you are having a dispute with the servicer, do not stop making your full payment each month. Consider carefully before putting another mortgage or lien on your home.

If you do not make your monthly mortgage payments, you will be in default on your loan. Foreclosure is a legal process in which a mortgaged property is sold to pay off the defaulted loan. If you find yourself facing foreclosure, there are steps that you should take. Contact your lender and be prepared to provide financial information. There may be a workout plan available to help you keep your home. There are also HUD-approved housing counseling agencies that are available to provide you information on and assistance in avoiding foreclosure. HUD's web site provides homeowners this information as well as other guidance in its "Guide to Avoiding Foreclosure" which can be found at http://www.hud.gov/foreclosure/.

Beware of scams! Watch out for equity skimming when a buyer offers to repay the mortgage or sell the property if you sign over the deed and move out. Be aware that there are phony counseling agencies that charge you a fee for the same services you can usually receive at no charge. Be sure to use only HUD-approved counseling agencies. Most importantly, NEVER sign anything that you have not read or do not understand.

X. Home Equity and Refinances

Home Equity Loan/Line of Credit

As you make payments on your mortgage loan or make improvements to your property, or if property values in your neighborhood increase, the equity in your home may increase. Home equity is the difference between your home's fair market value and the outstanding balances of all the loans and other liens on your property.

If you have equity in your property, you may be able to use it as collateral for a home equity loan or a home equity line of credit, often called a HELOC.

A closed-end home equity loan is for a fixed amount of money that you receive at closing. You will not be able to borrow additional money under the terms of this type of loan. An open-end home equity loan has a credit line set by the lender. With this loan you can choose when and how often to borrow money up to your credit limit.

Is a Home Equity Loan/Line of Credit Right For You?

You may want to make home improvements to increase the value of your home, or you may decide to consolidate your debts by paying off high-interest credit cards. Maybe you have unexpected medical bills or need funds to pay for school expenses. A home equity loan can be a convenient way to get money for these situations; however, before you get a home equity loan, there are things that you should carefully consider. Remember that a home equity loan creates another lien against your home and reduces the equity that you have built up. You could risk losing your home if you do not plan wisely.

Ask as many questions as you asked when you were looking for your home loan. The decision to get a home equity loan or line of credit should be made wisely. Make sure you can afford the loan. Have a solid financial plan and set up a budget, so you can be confident that you can make the additional monthly payment while still meeting your other financial obligations. You worked hard to get your home, don't risk losing it!

Additional assistance and guidance can be found in "What you should know about Home Equity Lines of Credit" published by the Federal Reserve Board. You can contact the Federal Reserve Board at the address and phone number provided in the Appendix at the end of this booklet for additional information.

Refinancing: Should You Consider Refinancing?

Refinancing is paying off one loan by obtaining another and is usually done to secure better loan terms such as a lower interest rate. You might also want to refinance for the same reasons you may have considered a home equity loan or line of credit - to get cash from the equity that you have built up in your home for such things as home improvements, paying off other debts, major purchases, starting a business, or education costs, etc.

You should carefully consider the terms of a refinance as well as the long-term impact on your financial situation. You should shop as carefully for your refinance loan as you did when you bought your home. Refinancing can deplete the equity you have built up if you take out the equity in your home in cash, and it can negatively affect your ability to pay your loan if you do not closely review the terms of your new loan. Consider the same issues that you addressed when you first applied for your home loan that have been discussed throughout this booklet.

On the positive side, if you shop carefully for your refinance, you could lower your monthly payments by getting a lower interest rate. Be wary of unsolicited refinancing offers that you may get in the mail or through e-mail. Although not all of these offers are deceptive, there are many unscrupulous loan originators who use the offers to find unsuspecting home owners. Some of these unscrupulous loan originators will even use the HUD and FHA logos in an attempt to make their solicitations appear legitimate. If you have any doubts about whether a communication has actually been sent by HUD, use the information in the Appendix to contact HUD.

XI. Appendix

ADDITIONAL INFORMATION

There are several federal laws which provide you with protection during the home buying process. The Equal Credit Opportunity Act ("ECOA") and the Fair Housing Act prohibit discrimination, and the Fair Credit Reporting Act ("FCRA") provides you with the right to certain credit information.

No Discrimination

ECOA prohibits lenders from discriminating against credit applicants in any aspect of credit transactions on the basis of race, color, religion, national origin, sex, marital status, age, the fact that all or part of the applicant's income comes from any public assistance program, or the fact that the applicant has exercised any right under any federal consumer credit protection law.

The Fair Housing Act prohibits housing discrimination because of race, color, religion, sex, disability, familial status or national origin. This prohibition applies, among other things, to the sale of a home to you, the making of loans for purchasing, constructing, improving, repairing or maintaining a dwelling, and the brokering and appraising of residential real estate.

If you feel you have been discriminated against by a lender or anyone else in the home buying process in violation of the Fair Housing Act, you can file a complaint at no cost with HUD. Following an investigation, if HUD determines that there is a reasonable cause to believe that your rights under the Fair Housing Act have been violated, it will issue a Charge of Discrimination on your behalf that will be adjudicated in administrative proceedings or in federal court. You may also file a complaint under ECOA with the Board of Governors of the Federal Reserve System or with an appropriate state agency under the state's equal credit opportunity laws.

You may also be able to file a private legal action or take other appropriate action if you are the victim of discrimination. You may wish to consult with an attorney to understand your rights.

Prompt Action/Notification of Action Taken

Your lender or mortgage broker must act on your application and inform you of the action taken no later than 30 days after it receives your completed application. Your application will not be considered complete, and the 30-day period will not begin, until you provide to your lender or mortgage broker all of the material and information requested.

Statement of Reasons for Denial

If your application is denied, ECOA requires your lender or mortgage broker to give you a statement of the specific reasons why it denied your application or tell you how you can obtain such a statement. The notice will also tell you which federal agency regulates the lender that denied your application so you can contact the agency if you believe it has illegally discriminated against you.

Obtaining Your Credit Report

The Fair Credit Reporting Act ("FCRA") requires a lender or mortgage broker that denies your loan application to tell you whether it based its decision on information contained in your credit report. If that information was a reason for the denial, the notice will tell you where you can get a free copy of the credit report. You have the right to dispute the accuracy or completeness of any information in your credit report. If you dispute any information, the credit reporting agency that prepared the report must investigate free of charge and notify you of the results of the investigation.

Obtaining Your Appraisal

The lender needs to know if the value of your home is enough to secure the loan. To get this information, the lender typically hires an appraiser, who gives a professional opinion about the value of your home. ECOA requires your lender or mortgage broker to tell you that you have a right to get a copy of the appraisal report. The notice will also tell you how and when you can ask for a copy.

HOEPA

If you ever decide to refinance your loan, or if you apply for a home equity installment loan, you should know about the Home Ownership and Equity Protection Act of 1994 (HOEPA). This law addresses certain unfair practices and establishes requirements for certain loans with high rates and fees. You can find out more information by contacting the Federal Trade Commission at the address and phone number listed in the Appendix.

DETERMINING WHAT YOU CAN AFFORD WORKSHEET

Use the worksheet below to calculate your monthly income and expenses to determine the amount you have left over every month to pay for house related expenses such as your monthly loan payment, property taxes and homeowner's insurance. There is also a mortgage calculator you may wish to use. It can be found at: http://www.ginniemae.gov/2_prequal/intro_questions.asp?Section=YPTH.

Determine Your Monthly Income and Expenses	Monthly Amount
Income (what you take home after taxes and other deductions)	
Borrower salary	$
Co-borrower salary	$
Other income	$
INCOME TOTAL	$
Expenses	
Credit cards	$
Car payment	$
Car insurance	$
Health insurance	$
Savings and retirement	$
Medical expenses	$
Child support and alimony	$
Tuition	$
Utilities	$
Clothing	$
Entertainment	$
Other expenses	$
EXPENSES TOTAL	$
TOTAL MONTHLY INCOME	$
SUBTRACT TOTAL MONTHLY EXPENSE	$
EQUALS	$

CONTACT INFORMATION

U.S. Department of Housing and Urban Development
451 7th Street, SW
Washington, DC 20410
202-708-1112
http://www.hud.gov

HUD's Office of RESPA and Interstate Land Sales
202-708-0502
http://www.hud.gov/respa

HUD Housing Counselors
1-800-569-4287 (Interactive system)
http://www.hud.gov/offices/hsg/sfh/hcc/hcs.cfm

HUD Foreclosure Prevention Information
http://www.hud.gov/foreclosure

Buying a HUD Home
http://www.hud.gov/offices/hsg/sfh/reo/reobuyfaq.cfm

FHA- Resource Center
1-800-CALL FHA (800-225-5342)
http://www.hud.gov/offices/hsg/sfh/fharesourcectr.cfm

Housing Discrimination Issues
Office of Fair Housing and Equal Opportunity
(See HUD address above)
1-202-708-1112
1-800-800-3088
http://portal.hud.gov/portal/page/portal/HUD/program_offices/fair_housing_equal_opp
To file a Housing Discrimination Complaint:
http://www.hud.gov/offices/fheo/online-complaint.cfm

Other Agencies

Truth in Lending Act, the Equal Credit Opportunity Act, adjustable rate mortgages, and home equity lines of credit
The Federal Reserve Board
Division of Consumer and
Community Affairs
20th and Constitution Avenue
Mail Stop 801
Washington DC 20551
202-452-3000
www.federalreserve.gov

Foreclosure Prevention Toolkit
Federal Deposit Insurance
Corporation
Division of Compliance
1730 Pennsylvania Ave
7th Floor
Washington DC 20429
877-275-3342
www.fdic.gov/consumers/loans/prevention/toolkit.html

VA-Guaranteed Loans
Department of Veterans Affairs
Consumer Affairs Service
810 Vermont Avenue, NW
Washington DC 20420
800-827-1000
www.va.gov

Rural Housing Loan Programs
Department of Agriculture
Rural Development/Rural Housing Services
Mail Stop MC-0701
1400 Independence Avenue, SW
Washington DC 20250
202-720-4581
www.rurdev.usda.gov

Home Ownership and Equity Protection Act of 1994 (HOEPA)
Federal Trade Commission
Consumer Response Center
600 Pennsylvania Avenue, N.W.
Washington DC 20580
877-382-4357
www.ftc.gov

GLOSSARY of TERMS

Appraiser: one who is trained and educated in the methods of determining the value of property (appraised value). You will pay a fee for an appraisal report containing an opinion as to the value of your property and the reasoning leading to this opinion.

Credit report fee: this fee covers the cost of a credit report which shows your credit history. The lender uses the information in a credit report to assess your credit worthiness.

Default: the inability to pay monthly mortgage payments in a timely manner or to otherwise meet the mortgage terms.

Delinquency: failure of a borrower to make timely mortgage payments under a loan agreement.

Down Payment: the portion of a home's purchase price that is paid in cash and is not part of the mortgage loan.

Earnest Money Deposit: money you will put down to show that you are serious about purchasing the home. It often becomes part of the down payment if the offer is accepted, is returned if the offer is rejected, or may be forfeited if you do not follow through with the deal.

Escrow Account: an impound account in which a portion of your monthly mortgage payment is deposited to cover annual charges for homeowner's insurance, mortgage insurance (if applicable), and property taxes.

Escrow Agent: a person or entity holding documents and funds in a transfer of real property, acting for both parties pursuant to instructions. Typically the agent is a person (often an attorney), escrow company or title company, depending on local practices.

Flood Certification Fee: a fee for the assessment of your property to determine if it is located in a flood prone area.

Foreclosure: a legal process in which mortgaged property is sold to pay the loan of the defaulting borrowers.

Good Faith Estimate (GFE): an estimate of the settlement charges you are likely to incur; it also contains other information about the loan.

Government Recording and Transfer Charges: fees for legally recording your deed and mortgage. These fees may be paid by you or by the seller depending upon the terms of the sales agreement.

Home Inspection: an inspection of the mechanical, electrical, and structural aspects of your home. You will pay a fee for this inspection, and the inspector will provide you a written report evaluating the condition of the home.

Homeowner's Insurance or Home Hazard Insurance: an insurance policy that protects your home and your possessions inside from serious loss, such as theft or fire. This insurance is usually required by all lenders to protect their investment and must be obtained before closing on your loan.

HUD-1 Settlement Statement: a statement that itemizes the services provided to you and the fees charged for those services. This form is filled out by the person who will conduct the settlement. You can ask to see your settlement statement at least one day prior to your settlement.

Interest: a fee charged by the lender for the use of its money.

Interest rate: the charge by the lender for borrowing money expressed as a percentage.

Lender Inspection Fees: this charge covers inspections, often of newly constructed housing, made by employees of your lender or by an outside inspector.

Loan to value (LTV) ratio: a percentage calculated by dividing the amount to be borrowed by the price or appraised value of the home to be purchased (whichever is less). The loan to value ratio is used to qualify borrowers for a mortgage, and the higher the LTV, the tighter the qualification guidelines for certain mortgage programs become. Low loan to value ratios are considered below 80%, and carry lower rates since borrowers are lower risk.

Mortgage: the transfer of an interest in property to a lender as a security for a debt. This interest may be transferred with a Deed of Trust in some states.

Origination Fee: a fee charged to the borrower by the loan originator for making a mortgage loan.

Origination Services: any service involved in the creation of a mortgage loan, including but not limited to the taking of the loan application, loan processing, and the underwriting and funding of loan, and the processing and administrative services required to perform these functions.

Payment Shock: a scenario in which monthly mortgage payments on an adjustable rate mortgage (ARM) rise so high that the borrower may not be able to afford the payments.

PITI: Principal, Interest, Taxes and Insurance: the four elements of a monthly mortgage payment; payments of principal and interest go directly towards repaying the loan while the portion that covers taxes and insurance goes into an escrow account to cover the fees when they are due.

Pest Inspection: an inspection for termites or other pest infestations of your home. This inspection is frequently required by your lender.

Point(s): amount of money paid to reduce the interest rate on a loan. A point is usually equal to 1% of the loan amount.

Pre-paid items: lenders often require the prepayment of items such as insurance premiums for private mortgage insurance, homeowner's insurance, and real estate taxes.

Prepayment Penalty: a fee charged if the mortgage loan is paid before the scheduled due date.

Private Mortgage Insurance (PMI): insurance that protects your lender if you default on your loan. With conventional loans, mortgage insurance is usually required if you do not make a down payment of at least 20% of your home's appraised value. Your lender may require payment of your first year's mortgage insurance premium or a lump sum premium that covers the life of the loan in advance at settlement. The same insurance protection on an FHA loan is called Mortgage Insurance Premium (MIP).

Recording and Transfer Charges: these charges include fees paid to the local government for filing official records of a real-estate transaction.

Sales Agreement: the contract signed by a buyer and the seller stating the terms and conditions under which a property will be sold. It may also be called an "Agreement of Sale" or "Purchase Contract."

Settlement: the time at which the property is formally sold and transferred from the seller to the buyer. It is at this time that the borrower takes on the loan obligation, pays all closing costs and receives title from the seller.

Settlement/Closing Agent: in some states, a settlement agent, or closing agent, handles the real estate transaction when you buy or sell a home. It may also be an attorney or a title agent. He or she oversees all legal documents, fee payments, and other details of transferring the property to ensure that the conditions of the contract have been met and appropriate real estate taxes have been paid.

Settlement Costs/Closing Costs: the customary costs above and beyond the sales price of the property that must be paid to cover the transfer of ownership at closing; these costs generally vary by geographic location and are typically detailed to the borrower at the time the GFE is given.

Survey Fee: a fee for obtaining a drawing of your property showing the location of the lot, any structures, and any encroachments. The survey fee is usually paid by the borrower.

Title Service Fees: title service fees include charges for title search and title insurance if required. This fee also includes the services of a title or settlement agent.

Title Insurance: insurance that protects your lender against any title dispute that may arise over your property. Through a title search, the lender verifies who the actual property-owners are and whether the property is free of liens. The title search company then issues title insurance which protects the title of the property against any unpaid mortgages and judgments. In case a claim is made against the property, the title insurance provides legal protection and pays for court fees and related costs. You may also purchase Owner's title insurance which protects you as the homeowner.

Tax certificate: official proof of payment of taxes due provided at the time of transfer of property title by the state or local government.

Tax Service Fee: this fee covers the cost of your lender engaging a third party to monitor and handle the payment of your property tax bills. This is done to ensure that your tax payments are made on time and to prevent tax liens from occurring.

Tolerance Category: the maximum amount by which the charges for a category or categories of settlement cost may exceed the amount of the estimate for such category or categories on a good faith estimate. When the originator selects and identifies the provider of services, these charges may only increase 10% in the aggregate. If the borrower selects a provider that is not on the written list provided by the loan originator, the lender is not subject to any tolerance restrictions for that service.

Types of Mortgage Loan Products

Adjustable Rate Mortgage (ARM): a mortgage loan or Deed of Trust which allows the lender to periodically adjust the interest rate in accordance with a specified index.

Balloon Mortgage: a balloon payment is due on a mortgage that usually offers a low monthly payment for an initial period of time. After that period of time elapses, the balance must be paid by the borrower or the amount must be refinanced. The large sum payable at the end of the loan term is called the "balloon payment."

Construction Loan: a short-term, interim loan for financing the cost of construction; the lender advances funds to the builder at periodic interval as work progresses.

Conventional Loan: a private sector loan which is not guaranteed or insured by the U.S. government.

Fixed-Rate Mortgage: a mortgage with an interest rate that does not change over the life of the loan, and as a result, monthly payments for principal and interest do not change.

Hybrid Arms: these loans are a mix or a hybrid of a fixed-rate period and an adjustable-rate period. For example, a 3/1 ARM will have a fixed interest rate for the first three years and then will adjust annually until the loan is paid off. The first number tells you how long the fixed interest-rate period will be and the second number tells you how often it will adjust after the initial period.

Interest Only ARMs: an interest-only (I-O) ARM payment plan allows you to pay only the interest for a specific number of years, typically between 3 and 10 years. This allows you to have smaller payments for a period of time. After that, your monthly payments will increase, even if the interest rate stays the same, because you must start paying back the principal as well as the interest each month.

OMB Approval No. 2502-0265

A. Settlement Statement (HUD-1)

B. Type of Loan

1. ☐ FHA	2. ☐ RHS	3. ☐ Conv. Unins.	6. File Number:	7. Loan Number:	8. Mortgage Insurance Case Number:
4. ☐ VA	5. ☐ Conv. Ins.				

C. Note: This form is furnished to give you a statement of actual settlement costs. Amounts paid to and by the settlement agent are shown. Items marked "(p.o.c.)" were paid outside the closing; they are shown here for informational purposes and are not included in the totals.

D. Name & Address of Borrower:	E. Name & Address of Seller:	F. Name & Address of Lender:

G. Property Location:	H. Settlement Agent:	I. Settlement Date:
	Place of Settlement:	

J. Summary of Borrower's Transaction / K. Summary of Seller's Transaction

J. Summary of Borrower's Transaction		K. Summary of Seller's Transaction	
100. Gross Amount Due from Borrower		**400. Gross Amount Due to Seller**	
101. Contract sales price		401. Contract sales price	
102. Personal property		402. Personal property	
103. Settlement charges to borrower (line 1400)		403.	
104.		404.	
105.		405.	
Adjustment for items paid by seller in advance		**Adjustment for items paid by seller in advance**	
106. City/town taxes to		406. City/town taxes to	
107. County taxes to		407. County taxes to	
108. Assessments to		408. Assessments to	
109.		409.	
110.		410.	
111.		411.	
112.		412.	
120. Gross Amount Due from Borrower		**420. Gross Amount Due to Seller**	
200. Amount Paid by or in Behalf of Borrower		**500. Reductions In Amount Due to seller**	
201. Deposit or earnest money		501. Excess deposit (see instructions)	
202. Principal amount of new loan(s)		502. Settlement charges to seller (line 1400)	
203. Existing loan(s) taken subject to		503. Existing loan(s) taken subject to	
204.		504. Payoff of first mortgage loan	
205.		505. Payoff of second mortgage loan	
206.		506.	
207.		507.	
208.		508.	
209.		509.	
Adjustments for items unpaid by seller		**Adjustments for items unpaid by seller**	
210. City/town taxes to		510. City/town taxes to	
211. County taxes to		511. County taxes to	
212. Assessments to		512. Assessments to	
213.		513.	
214.		514.	
215.		515.	
216.		516.	
217.		517.	
218.		518.	
219.		519.	
220. Total Paid by/for Borrower		**520. Total Reduction Amount Due Seller**	
300. Cash at Settlement from/to Borrower		**600. Cash at Settlement to/from Seller**	
301. Gross amount due from borrower (line 120)		601. Gross amount due to seller (line 420)	
302. Less amounts paid by/for borrower (line 220)	( )	602. Less reductions in amounts due seller (line 520)	( )
303. Cash ☐ From ☐ To Borrower		**603. Cash ☐ To ☐ From Seller**	

The Public Reporting Burden for this collection of information is estimated at 35 minutes per response for collecting, reviewing, and reporting the data. This agency may not collect this information, and you are not required to complete this form, unless it displays a currently valid OMB control number. No confidentiality is assured; this disclosure is mandatory. This is designed to provide the parties to a RESPA covered transaction with information during the settlement process.

Previous edition are obsolete   Page 1 of 3   HUD-1

L. Settlement Charges

700. Total Real Estate Broker Fees	Paid From Borrower's Funds at Settlement	Paid From Seller's Funds at Settlement
Division of commission (line 700) as follows :		
701. $ to		
702. $ to		
703. Commission paid at settlement		
704.		

800. Items Payable in Connection with Loan		
801. Our origination charge $ (from GFE #1)		
802. Your credit or charge (points) for the specific interest rate chosen $ (from GFE #2)		
803. Your adjusted origination charges (from GFE #A)		
804. Appraisal fee to (from GFE #3)		
805. Credit report to (from GFE #3)		
806. Tax service to (from GFE #3)		
807. Flood certification to (from GFE #3)		
808.		
809.		
810.		
811.		

900. Items Required by Lender to be Paid in Advance		
901. Daily interest charges from to @ $ /day (from GFE #10)		
902. Mortgage insurance premium for months to (from GFE #3)		
903. Homeowner's insurance for years to (from GFE #11)		
904.		

1000. Reserves Deposited with Lender		
1001. Initial deposit for your escrow account (from GFE #9)		
1002. Homeowner's insurance months @ $ per month $		
1003. Mortgage insurance months @ $ per month $		
1004. Property Taxes months @ $ per month $		
1005. months @ $ per month $		
1006. months @ $ per month $		
1007. Aggregate Adjustment -$		

1100. Title Charges		
1101. Title services and lender's title insurance (from GFE #4)		
1102. Settlement or closing fee $		
1103. Owner's title insurance (from GFE #5)		
1104. Lender's title insurance $		
1105. Lender's title policy limit $		
1106. Owner's title policy limit $		
1107. Agent's portion of the total title insurance premium to $		
1108. Underwriter's portion of the total title insurance premium to $		
1109.		
1110.		
1111.		

1200. Government Recording and Transfer Charges		
1201. Government recording charges (from GFE #7)		
1202. Deed $ Mortgage $ Release $		
1203. Transfer taxes (from GFE #8)		
1204. City/County tax/stamps Deed $ Mortgage $		
1205. State tax/stamps Deed $ Mortgage $		
1206.		

1300. Additional Settlement Charges		
1301. Required services that you can shop for (from GFE #6)		
1302. $		
1303. $		
1304.		
1305.		

1400. Total Settlement Charges (enter on lines 103, Section J and 502, Section K)		

Comparison of Good Faith Estimate (GFE) and HUD-1 Charrges		Good Faith Estimate	HUD-1
Charges That Cannot Increase	**HUD-1 Line Number**		
Our origination charge	# 801		
Your credit or charge (points) for the specific interest rate chosen	# 802		
Your adjusted origination charges	# 803		
Transfer taxes	# 1203		

Charges That In Total Cannot Increase More Than 10%		Good Faith Estimate	HUD-1
Government recording charges	# 1201		
	#		
	#		
	#		
	#		
	#		
	#		
	#		
Total			
Increase between GFE and HUD-1 Charges		$ or	%

Charges That Can Change		Good Faith Estimate	HUD-1
Initial deposit for your escrow account	# 1001		
Daily interest charges $ /day	# 901		
Homeowner's insurance	# 903		
	#		
	#		
	#		

Loan Terms

Your initial loan amount is	$
Your loan term is	years
Your initial interest rate is	%
Your initial monthly amount owed for principal, interest, and any mortgage insurance is	$ includes ☐ Principal ☐ Interest ☐ Mortgage Insurance
Can your interest rate rise?	☐ No ☐ Yes, it can rise to a maximum of % . The first change will be on and can change again every after . Every change date, your interest rate can increase or decrease by %. Over the life of the loan, your interest rate is guaranteed to never be lower than % or higher than %.
Even if you make payments on time, can your loan balance rise?	☐ No ☐ Yes, it can rise to a maximum of $
Even if you make payments on time, can your monthly amount owed for principal, interest, and mortgage insurance rise?	☐ No ☐ Yes, the first increase can be on and the monthly amount owed can rise to $. The maximum it can ever rise to is $.
Does your loan have a prepayment penalty?	☐ No ☐ Yes, your maximum prepayment penalty is $
Does your loan have a balloon payment?	☐ No ☐ Yes, you have a balloon payment of $ due in years on
Total monthly amount owed including escrow account payments	☐ You do not have a monthly escrow payment for items, such as property taxes and homeowner's insurance. You must pay these items directly yourself. ☐ You have an additional monthly escrow payment of $ that results in a total initial monthly amount owed of $. This includes principal, interest, any mortgage insurance and any items checked below: ☐ Property taxes ☐ Homeowner's insurance ☐ Flood insurance ☐ ☐ ☐

Note: If you have any questions about the Settlement Charges and Loan Terms listed on this form, please contact your lender.

THE DO LIST

- Shop for your loan.
- Interview real estate agents, mortgage brokers, lenders and other settlement service providers to find the best professionals for your loan and settlement needs.
- Be sure to read and understand everything before you sign anything.
- Accurately report your debts.
- Be honest about all sources of funds you will use to purchase your home.
- Be upfront about any credit problems you have or have had in the past.
- Be wary of unsolicited loan or refinance offers that you receive in the mail or through e-mail.
- Always pay your mortgage payment on time, even if you are having a dispute with your loan servicer.
- If you are having problems paying your mortgage, contact your loan servicer immediately.

THE DON'T LIST

- Do not sign blank documents.
- Do not overstate your income.
- Do not overstate your length of employment.
- Do not overstate your assets.
- Do not change your income tax returns.
- Do not list fake co-borrowers on your loan application.
- Do not provide false documentation or permit someone to provide false documents about you.

www.ingramcontent.com/pod-product-compliance
Lightning Source LLC
Chambersburg PA
CBHW081236170526

45165CB00009B/3069

9781500621452